C000142672

FOR WOMEN: MORE MONOLOGUES THEY HAVEN'T HEARD

Susan Pomerance

Dramaline Publications

Copyright © 1995, Dramaline Publications.

All Rights Reserved.

Printed in the United States of America.

No part of this publication may be reproduced or transmitted in any form or by any means, electronic or mechanical, including photocopy, recording, or any information storage and retrieval system now known or to be invented, without permission in writing from the publisher, except by a reviewer who wishes to quote brief passages in connection with a review written for inclusion in a magazine, newspaper, or for broadcast. Material in this publication may be utilized for workshop, audition, and classwork purposes without royalty consideration. If, however, the material is presented individually, or in total, before an audience where admission is charged, royalty payment is required. Contact the publisher for applicable rates.

Dramaline Publications 36-851 Palm View Road
Rancho Mirage, CA 92270
Phone 619/770-6076 Fax 619/770-4507

Library of Congress Cataloging-in-Publication Data

Pomerance, Susan.
        For women: more monologues they haven't heard/Susan Pomerance.
        p.   cm.
        ISBN-940669-33-1 (alk. paper)
        1. Monologues. 2. Acting.   3. Women—Drama.   I. Title.
PN2080.P66 1995
812' .045089287—dc20   95-25807

Cover art: John Sabel

This book is printed on 55# Glatfelter acid-free paper, a paper that meets the requirements of the American Standard of Permanence of paper for printed library material.

CONTENTS

INTRODUCTION

While sitting here contemplating the fast-approaching Western Pennsylvania autumnal season, Rolling Rock beer, and pizza, I've decided to write an introduction to this book. This will be a first. I haven't written introductions to my earlier Dramaline books. I guess this is because so much has already been written by so many on the subject. But, upon reflection, perhaps this is the reason I feel it necessary to contribute to the ever-expanding pile.

Much of the material written relative to the proper presentation to dramatic work is, I feel, overstated and overblown. It smacks of the academic rather than dealing with the key ingredient—passion. And by passion I certainly don't mean emoting while flailing about the stage or set with expansive gestures. God, don't we have enough of this in our films and TV work? It's so seldom that we see restrained acting, where the emotion is contained but projected. Take anger, for example. It is obviously the vogue to show anger by over-the-top ranting, wildness of eye, and gnashing of teeth. How maddening.

The other evening I was watching an actor whose work embodied truth of character, emotional restraint, and passion. It was Joss Ackland in the film *White Mischief.* It is textbook work in the art of truthful acting. Although his character is seething with hatred and frustration, Ackland never overplays. But you can feel his animus. It's there, boiling up out of his character, and it's powerful and frightening. And it is made more powerful because it isn't displayed by wild gestures, tantrums, and ear-splitting harangue. It's wonderful. The man is a veritable volcano, but he never overflows. Rent it.

Restrained passion is the key. An actress friend of mine once told me something I've never forgotten. She said, "You gotta go nuts." And I knew exactly what she meant. She meant that every fiber of your energy and intelligence must be focused. And this applies to all art: dance, painting, poetry—you name it. Great art demands going crazy. But it should never show in an overt way. It should be underlying and controlled. The most difficult work should appear effortless. The novice should look at great art and say, "Hey, I could do that." Oh yeah, wanna bet?

This is certainly not hard and fast advice. But I believe it, so, what the hell, I may as well inject my two cents worth. Besides, what would an introduction be without a little pedantic rambling?

Here is a tip that may help you in preparing your monologues for presentation. Sir Winston Churchill was meticulous in the preparation and presentation to his speeches. Even though they may have seemed gloriously extemporaneous, they were painstakingly crafted and rehearsed. And before they were delivered, he had them set in "speech" or "psalm" form. Here is a sample of the dramatic arrangement of the speech Churchill delivered to the House of Commons after Hitler became absolute master of the Third Reich:

I have on more than one occasion
 Made my appeal that the Führer of Germany
  Should become the Hitler of peace.

When a man is fighting in a desperate conflict,
 He may have to grind his teeth and flash his eyes;
  Anger and hatred nerve the arm of strife.

But success should bring a mellow, genial air
 And, by altering the mood to suit the new circumstances,
  Preserve and consolidate in tolerance and goodwill
   What has been gained by conflict.

Arranged thus, his words gave an illusion of spontaneity. His notes also contained stage directions ("pause; grope for word" and "stammer; correct self"). Each of his speeches was a dramatic, vibrant occasion.

With this in mind, I have here arranged in dramatic form the first few lines of Mariah's speech on page one. Hopefully this example will aid you in arranging your monologues for maximum dramatic impact.

MARIAH

(*She reflects; begins slowly*)

It's gotten to the point where . . . the days come and go without meaning.

    The same old boring grind (*pick up cadence*)

      And the months pass

        And before you know it,

          Here you are (*brief pause*),

            Up to your ass in yesterdays.

(*Again slowly*)

    And then it's too late

      Because you've let your chances slip you by.

        And, like, here you are (*pause; looking off wistfully*)

        Stuck and sinking fast.

Susan Pomerance
Bryn Mawr, Pennsylvania
September 1995

MARIAH

It is evening, and the day is fast dying in a small Midwestern town. Mariah stands at her bedroom window, looking out over rolling hills. She reflects upon lost loves and squandered opportunities.

It's gotten to the point where the days come and go without meaning. The same old boring grind. And the months pass, and before you know it, here you are, up to your ass in yesterdays. And then it's too late because you've let your chances slip you by. And, like, here you are . . . stuck and sinking fast.

And who do I have to blame for being up to my neck in quicksand? My parents? My friends? Bad breaks? Nope, I have myself to blame because I'm the one who couldn't get off the dime and make decisions at the crossroads. And I've had lots of promising crossroads, too. Like Ned Garner. He wanted to get married and move to St. Louis. But I couldn't make up my mind. I'd miss my friends, I'd miss my family, I hated St. Louis. So I took a pass. And so did Ned. Today he's married with three kids and is the CEO of a big plastics company. The last time he came home for a visit, he was driving a Mercedes the size of a 747. Then there was David Greenbaum. He was nuts about me, but I thought he only liked me because I was a WASP and that he only wanted me for my body because it reminded him of the white meat of chicken. So I screwed around and screwed around till he got fed up and married Sally Richardson. Today they have homes in Aspen and Palm Beach, because David invented a slicer that slices vegetables so thin you can read the Oxford Dictionary through them. My luck, the story of my life.

Then there was the opportunity I had with Ralston Purina. Their regional manager thought I was the greatest thing since oat bran. Still does. And if I do say so myself, when it comes to this industry, I'm on top of it. Anyway, he offered me a fantastic job with the company. Again I vacillated. I didn't think it'd be fair to my father. He leans on me for everything. So in my convoluted wisdom, I turned down *this* opportunity, too. The person who took the job is today VP of sales with a six-figure salary. And these are just a few examples of blown chances. My track record in "the making the right decisions department" is miserable.

So here I am, still managing my father's feed mill, unmarried, with a boy riend about as exciting as cold Cream O' Wheat, with no legitimate prospects on the immediate horizon. In fact, when I look out over the horizon all I see is the sun setting on a life of missed opportunities and a sky full of vegetable slicers.

JOYCE

She doesn't tan, she blisters. While her friends get golden, she gets magenta. At the moment, she can't even sit comfortably due to a day at the beach. Mr. Sol is definitely not Janet's friend. Here, due to extreme sunburn, she rejects the advances of her lover, bemoans the state of her lobster-like body and the fact that she can't tan.

Don't touch me! Jesus Christ, whatever you do, don't touch me! Do you want to burn your dick? (*Beat.*) You think I'm kidding? I'm on fire everywhere. You wear a thong, you pay the price because the sun finds its way into the nooks and crannies. I should have known better. I've never tanned. Ever. Because I'm cursed with the skin of an albino. The poet Anne Sexton wrote that sunbathing was "like having intercourse with God." Well, for me it's like crawling in bed with the devil.

(*Beat.*) No! Forget it! I don't care how careful you'll be. Unless you've figured out some mystical way of doing me without us touching. Just put your hormones on back-order for a few days, okay?

Look at me. Look! I'm a walking beet with freckles. Why me? Everybody else I know gets, like, this gorgeous tan. Like, Stephanie Loretti. She passes under a sixty-watt bulb, she looks like Zorba the Greek. It's that goddamn thick, Neapolitan skin. I'll bet she can't even cut herself. And Ada, she gets this great golden tan in twenty minutes. But me, what do I get? I get to turn into frijoles. Then there's the pain and the peeling. (*Beat.*) Why don't I give it up? Because I wanna be a tanned person who looks drop-dead beautiful in summer colors.

I don't get it. My mother tans, my father tans, my brother tans, even my little brat cousins get brown enough to join a minstrel show. But me, shit! I get vermilion and peel like a snake. (*Beat.*) I've tried that. For most people, tanning booths are cool. For me, they're murder. They turn me into steak tartare. I might as well go sit on a barbecue.

(*Exposing her back.*) Look at my back. Is this red, or what? And hot? A firewalker couldn't run across it. (*Beat.*) Yes, of course I've tried Paba. But what the hell's the point? Who wants to sit in the sun all day and still wind up looking like a vampire? I want color. (*Beat.*) Oh, yeah, I've gone through all the self-tanning junk on the market: Coppertone, Hawaiian Tropic, Lancôme—you name it. Maybe for some people it's okay. For me—disaster. It turns me this horrible color, makes me look like a big orange popsickle. And I can't seem to get it on evenly. And it has this odd smell, like scorched hair.

When I asked my dermatologist, he said it has to do with a lack of melanin. Then he goes and throws in this bullshit cliché, "There is no such thing as a healthy tan." Who cares if it's healthy? I don't give a damn. I'll take the risk, because everybody looks better with a nice, even suntan. People look twice. Like George Hamilton. A tan's made his career because it takes your mind off the fact he can't act. (*Reacting to the pain.*) Ouch! Damn . . . I'm on fire . . . I'm dying!

Look, I don't care how horny you are. Right now all I wanna do is go sit on ice. (*Beat.*) When? I don't know. In a few days. Maybe Sunday, after I get back from the beach.

LOLA

*She was born in a rural community. Now she is a successful reales-
tate broker in a major metropolitan market. But the pressures atten-
dant to her success are taking their toll, and the resulting stress is
having deleterious effects. As we join her monologue, she is writing
an ad for a new listing.*

(*Writing.*) "Situated on beautiful Washington Park with a view that
goes on and on, this . . . " No—I hate that! (*She erases.*)

(*Writing.*) " . . . with a view of forever, this four-bedroom, three-
bath, two-story home is in perfect condition. Loaded with . . ." No,
hell no! I've said this a thousand times. Damn! I'm so sick and tired
of writing this trite crap. How about this for a change? This should
get their attention. "If you're interested in a four-bedroom, three-
bath, two-story, over-priced piece of shit, this is the home for you.
(*Stabs a period to the paper. Sits back momentarily with a look of
satisfaction. She continues her writing.*) "Only a short distance from
the inner-city, you'll be serenaded by the phony moans of working
hookers, and the percussive sounds of gang warfare." (*She throws
down her pen in disgust and turns toward the audience.*)

I can't write any more of this tripe. I've had it. For eight years
I've been dreaming up fantasies to capture the imagination of the potential home buyer. I've created some of the wildest fiction ever.
Hell, Jules Verne couldn't do better. I've turned lean-tos into man-
sions, termite-infested rat traps into castles. But . . . hell, I just can't
write this crap anymore. You reach a point, you know. Like with
anything else that you've done to death.

I don't know what's going on. It's just . . . my heart's not in it
anymore, I guess. Used to be, I was like a shark, you know. Always
maneuvering, always on the prowl, always moving ahead with this

killer instinct. I mean, this is what it takes to be a successful salesperson. Aggressiveness, twenty-four hours a day. High-energy.

This was my dream when I came here from Westerville. To be *somebody*. And I've succeeded. I mean . . . the Millionaires' Club three years in a row. Hey, you don't get gold pins in your lapel for sitting on your butt. And financially, I'm doing really good. But emotionally lately—the pits. Because I'm always pushing, always achieving, always conniving, constantly promoting with no time for relaxation, friends, or a decent relationship. Successful brokers never sleep.

I think the realities hit me when I went back home last month. Suddenly, the place looked different to me. It didn't depress me the way it used to when I was younger. In fact, there was this . . . this serenity about the place. One afternoon I walked up the hill above my folks' house and looked out over the valley. It was *so* quiet. And that weekend, for the first time in months, I didn't have a migraine. And then there were my friends, the girls I put down for selling out to cookie baking and carpet rats. They all seemed to be so damn happy. And not a single one of them has a gold pin. (*Beat.*) Oh, well. (*She turns again to her writing, approaching the task with an air of resignation. She writes.*) "Priced at only $495,000, this beauty won't last. Call today for a private showing . . . "

CINDI

It's not that she didn't know that Tony had other girlfriends. After all, they're both adults, and they have had past relationships. But what she wasn't prepared for were repeated contacts with a former lover. Here she attempts to clear the air with regard to these contacts and Tony's apparent need to maintain them.

Look, I know you've had other women. I've had other men. We knew this going in, okay? (*Beat.*) Wait a minute . . . let me finish. (*Beat.*) Will you please shut up for a minute? What I'm trying to say is, I'm not on the phone with Roger every goddamned day of the week. Roger and I are history. But you and Diane. What the hell is this, anyway? Here you are talking to her again this morning. (*Beat.*) Crossword puzzle? Bullshit! She could call the nine-hundred number. It was just an excuse to call. Besides, you talked to her for twenty minutes. It doesn't take that long to come up with a four-letter word for whatever. (*Beat.*) I'm not buying it, okay? Yesterday you talked to her for forty-five minutes. I took a walk, and when I came back you were still on the phone. (*Beat.*) So what? So she got dumped on by her boyfriend. Big deal. She's the one who called it quits with you, in case you've forgotten. She unloaded on you good, mister. Christ, she was running around on you for months. This is not a nice person here, Tony, this is a bitch. And now she calls up with this drowning-bird act and you go for it like some overweening jerk. I can't believe it.

(*Beat.*) You couldn't be rude. C'mon. I can understand it—barely—maybe one time, okay? One time! But she's been calling you three and four times a week. And what pisses me off more than anything is that you either don't want to—or you haven't got the balls to—tell her to knock it off. (*Beat.*) No, no, no—please. Spare me here, okay? She's not hurting. No way. She's just sorry she treated you like crap and lost you and now she wants to weasel her way back into your life. You can't see this? How would you feel if Roger started calling me every day? (*Beat.*) Oh yeah, how's it different? It's different because I'm a woman, right? Bullshit! And if he did call, I'd get rid of him firmly but politely; I'd cut it off.

And how about this latest ploy of hers? Asking you if you want to come by her place to pick up some books you left. How about this for fucking nerve? With me sitting here listening. How the hell do you think this makes me feel? Don't you think I deserve better than this? (*Beat.*) What? You don't see anything wrong with it. Are you kidding here? Am I hearing you right, is this you talking, or is there somebody else in the room? I mean, do you really think that I'm going to put up with . . . (*She is interrupted by the telephone's ring. She goes to the phone and answers.*) Hello. Oh, hello Diane . . . Tony? No, he isn't here right now. He's out looking for an apartment. (*She slams the receiver.*)

SUZANNE

Suzanne's husband, Robert, was a loving, caring partner, supportive of her and her children's needs. Their family life and relationship was ideal. Until that fateful day when her daughter informed her that Robert's attentions toward her far exceeded fatherhood.

I guess there's no way of ever knowing. Robert always seemed so "normal." I'd known him since college, since we were freshmen at Michigan State. We had the same interests, the same background. In fact, we were from the same home town—Dearborn. He was very athletic, loved sports, was the epitome of the well-adjusted, American male. There was nothing in his make-up that would indicate that he was. . . . But, then again, how do you ever know? It's a buried thing, an emotional cancer.

Sexually there was nothing to indicate that he had aberrant desires. Sex between us was always an open, fulfilling thing. Looking back, I can't recall ever sensing that he was harboring latent tendencies. Like I said, he always seemed so damned "normal."

We were married after graduating from college. We moved back to Dearborn, where Robert took a job with Ford, and I hooked up with a data-processing group out of Toledo. Shortly after, I became pregnant and gave birth to our first daughter, Sherry. Then, two years later, along came Diane. Things couldn't have been better. We had the ideal marriage. We were both doing well in our jobs, the money was rolling in, the future looked fantastic. And at our tenth anniversary, we were apparently sitting on top of the world. Until March of this year.

I guess I was either too busy, or too complacent, to see the signs. I just thought Sherry was going through a "phase." You know, listlessness, moodiness, shutting herself away in her room after school—the standard behavior for kids her age, right? But in time I sensed there was more to it. Especially after she broke down crying a couple of times for no apparent reason. When I confronted her, she was evasive. Then, it came out. Robert had been molesting her for years.

I couldn't believe it. I didn't *want* to believe it. I accused her of lying, or making it up for some vengeful reason. Instead of being sympathetic, I was defensive of Robert. But it was inescapable. She was too believable, her details, her attitude, her stories were too credible. God, I can't tell you the emotions. It was like a personal invasion. I was sickened beyond anything I can put into words. The man I'd been sleeping with for years, my husband, was . . . with his own child, his own flesh and blood . . . his *daughter*!

When I confronted him, he denied everything. He put it back on Sherry. She was fantasizing, she was lying, she resented our relationship. But it wouldn't wash. I knew, and he knew I knew.

I've heard of cases when couples work it out. Therapy, psychiatry—whatever. But for me, it was over. No therapy would ever erase that fact that he's a deceitful, child-molesting sonofabitch. And there was no way I would ever want this man near my daughters again. And I'll fight to keep him as far away as possible.

It's been a sickening, devasting experience. In time, perhaps, I'll get over it. I just hope I can say the same for Sherry.

LOUISE

This speech requires two scenes. The first at her girlfriend's home over coffee, the second at her gynecologist's office. In the former she expresses serious trepidation with respect to pregnancy, in the later she reflects disappointment that her tests are negative.

Scene One.

For you it was never a problem. All you ever wanted was to get married, settle down, and have a litter of children. There was never any doubt. You're the full-time mother type, Jan, always were. You were cut out for it. Me? I'm not so sure. You have to give up too much. I know this sounds selfish, but the thought of the whole pregnancy thing is depressing. I mean, all this garbage with gaining a couple of dress sizes, check-ups, morning sickness, waddling around like a duck for months. . . . (*Beat.*) Yeah, well for you maybe the time passes quickly. Like I said, you're a born mother machine. And then . . . then the kid. *This* is the scary part. Jan, I'm not crazy about having this baby. (*Beat.*) I know it sounds awful, but this is how I feel, okay? Why fake it?

(*Beat.*) Jim? He thinks it's wonderful, he's already bought a box of cigars. Easy for him. Big deal. He doesn't have to lie there spread-eagle while they pull a watermelon through a keyhole. And that's another thing—the pain. (*She shivers at the thought. Beat.*) Great, Jan, very reassuring. It only lasts for a few seconds. So does a fatal heart attack. Please, no more of the maternity-ward psychology, okay?

Then there's the responsibility connected with raising children. And the expense. I don't have to tell you what it costs. Look at you, strapped half the time because you've got a house full of famished wolves. And what's the last time you've gone out and bought a decent outfit? And what about schooling? Do you know what it costs to put a kid through college these days? The only way you'll be able to stay out of the poor house is to convince your children to take up welding. (*Beat.*) Okay, for you it's a blessing. Wonderful. I'm thrilled for you. But for me the thought of the whole thing is a real downer. And I don't want to give up my job. I like what I'm doing.

(*Beat.*) Maybe, but I doubt it. I'm as regular as clockwork. The "P" word's written all over me. I guess this is the payback for an orgasm.

Scene Two. Her gynecologist's office, a few days later.

I'm not? You're kidding? But . . . two periods. I mean . . . I had all the symptoms. I felt pregnant. I felt like a walking mountain of fertility. (*Beat.*) You're sure, you're absolutely certain? (*Beat.*) You're sure there isn't some kind of mix-up? I mean, it happens all the time on TV. (*Beat.*) I'll be damned. (*Beat.*) No, no . . . I'm okay, I'm fine. It's just that . . . I mean . . . it's kind of a letdown, you know.

I mean . . . a child, a baby. I didn't think I'd care, but all of a sudden, and I can't explain it, all of a sudden, for some reason, I'm disappointed. (*Beat.*) Yes, I'm sure it's a normal reaction. Funny, isn't it? I wasn't even sure I wanted a baby. In fact, I resented being pregnant, being—whatever. But now . . . I mean . . .

God, excuse me, but I almost feel like crying.

LESLIE

Her father-in-law pays unannounced visits when her husband is out of town on business matters. And his interests are more than familial. In the interest of internal harmony, she has endured these embarrassing interludes, and has artfully fended his untoward advances. Finally her patience has been exhausted. In this scene, she administers the coup de grâce to the situation.

Stop! Don't move! Don't come a step closer! Don't even think about it! (*Beat.*) You heard me, I'm not kidding! I've put up with this non-sense for too long, and now it's over. Over, do you hear me, Roy? I want you to leave now. Right now! And if you don't, you're going to be one sorry bastard. I've had it. And if you persist, I'm not going to give a damn who hears what, or who's hurt, or who's offended. All I know is that these visits have just become history.

I've put up with your crap because I don't want to create a scene in the family. Because, if at all possible, I want to spare people hurt and embarrassment. Just how do you think your son would take the news that his father is coming on to his wife? (*Beat.*) Oh, you haven't, huh? Oh, really? Just what do you call these unexpected visits every time Phil's out of town? You sure as hell aren't dropping by to sample my brownies. And what about the sexual innuendoes, and the coming up behind me and rubbing me. (*Beat.*) Affection, hell! You think a woman doesn't know when there's something else behind it?

I thought by the way I've rejected your advances you'd get the drift. I thought you'd pick up on the fact your behavior makes my skin crawl. I thought you'd come to terms with this and exercise some kind of propriety. But no, you're either too stupid or emotionally hot-wired to the point that good manners mean nothing. (*Beat.*) You're shocked? Please. You're unshockable. You have no manners, no subtlety, no restraint. You're an old lecher, Roy, an old, indiscreet fool who's risking blowing a family apart because you've deluded yourself into thinking you're a roué.

The sick thing about this is that it's family. This doesn't bother you? The fact that I'm your daughter-in-law, the mother of your grandchildren? And what about your wife? If Helen knew about this, it'd kill her. Haven't you given this any thought? Haven't you stopped to consider the seriousness of your actions? (*Beat.*) Oh, I wouldn't, would I? Well, just keep up this craziness and you'll see what I'll do.

Now I want you to leave. I want you to get out of here immediately and never come back again when Phil's away—ever. If you leave now, and promise never approach me again, I'll forget about your little visits—they never happened. But if you persist, if you continue to let your crotch run away with your brain, I'll expose you for what you are: a lecherous, incestuous sonofabitch.

Now get the fuck out of my house!

GRACE

Grace is a manicurist in a beauty salon in Aspen, Colorado. She works long hours to support herself, her son, and her mother who babysits for the child. The complications of being a single, working mother are manifest in this monologue.

(*Confiding to a customer as she works.*) I get in here a little before eight. I drive in from Carbondale. Sometimes, in the winter, I have to leave home around seven. The roads, you know. This place is Siberia most of the year. During the season, I work sometimes ten, twelve hours a day. This is when the town is crawling with the rich and famous. It's also the time you get the biggest tips. Barbie Benton gave me a hundred dollars last Christmas. Very generous.

I've been doing this for about five years. I had to do something. I was pregnant, and when my boyfriend found out, he took off for California. I haven't seen him since. Don't want to. It was a low point for me. Here I was, basically uneducated, pregnant, and alone. I had no prospects—nothing. Thank God my mother let me move back in with her. She'd been living by herself for years. Ever since my dad decided to become a full-time jerk. I went to beauty school in Denver and decided that doing nails was my thing. When a friend told me about an opening here, I jumped at it. This is a good shop, and Aspen's a hot little city. Lots of action, lots of money. I work on people from all over the world.

I get along pretty good and can afford to support my mother and my son. I'm lucky my mom sits for Josh. If she didn't, I'd have to put him in a day school. I don't like those places. I think they mess children up. I mean, how good can a kid feel about himself when his mom drops him off like a bundle of mail every day? I don't care what they say, I think it leaves a mark.

Not that this is the best situation. The best is, like, being able to stay home, be a full-time mother. With a father in the house. And, a lot of time, there's tension between my mother and me. She's a good person, but she goes overboard with the discipline. She's deep into this eye-for-an-eye religion, and it worries me because of Josh. She's very big on guilt. We get into it about this. But I can't say too much, because I'm kind of, like, in a helpless position here, you know. I mean, as long as she's with Josh all day while I'm working, there isn't a lot I can do. I'm just hoping that she doesn't mess up his mind with all the God-fearing stuff.

Some nights, I don't get out of here till after eight. By the time I get back to Carbondale, Josh is in bed, and Mom's watching the sitcoms. I grab some leftovers, and watch the news, and it's time for bed. This is pretty much the routine. It's kind of boring, and some nights when I'm sitting there with my mother watching TV I get, like, this empty feeling inside. It's, like . . . I dunno, it's kind of like, like . . . there's got to be something more, you know.

BRENDA

She's in misery from head to toe from the daily aerobics classes that she attends at her boyfriend's insistence. But she has had it.

I can't take it anymore. My ankles are turning to rubber. Up, down, up, down, across, back, forward, jump. (*Beat.*) I don't give a damn what the experts say, this isn't proper exercise for humans. This routine is for chimps.

(*Beat.*) Look, I don't care if I'm paid up for a year. I'm out of here. I'm not continuing to torture myself with these stupid, high-impact, aerobics classes. I don't like coming over here, I hate getting up early in the morning, and I don't like people with attitude; like most of the women in the class. (*Beat.*) C'mon, wake up. They're arrogant bitches who are body conscious to the point of mental stultification. (*Beat.*) I know they're in great shape, this isn't the question. I know a great butt when I see one. I also can spot a phony in a Range Rover, talking on her cellular and drinking Evian. So . . . I'm out.

(*Beat.*) I don't care if you continue. What's it to me? You love it. You like jumping around to music you can hear all the way to Moscow. And you're not alone. The aerobics thing is very popular. So what? So are Big Macs. This has nothing to do with you. If you enjoy it—enjoy it. But for me . . . I'd rather slide nude down a cactus. After I got out of here yesterday, I was so sore I couldn't smile. Swear to God. I thought exercise was supposed to make you feel better. Before I started this silly shit, I felt fantastic. Now my hip aches, my knees hurt, my back's a mess, and I'm going to go broke buying Anacin.

It takes a certain kind of body for this kind of pounding. A body like the girl in the front row has. She has no weight. She has the density of a potato chip. What does she weigh, eighty pounds? Maybe. And this is in good shape? You ever check out her legs?

They look like pipe cleaners. This is the reason she can gyrate like a monkey on a spring for an hour. You either have to be built like a skeleton or like a UPS truck. Have thighs on you like Sequoias. Frankly, I don't find this attractive. This is nothing I would aspire to. You can't actually think these people are feminine. (*Beat.*) Okay, so you can appreciate what they've done with their bodies. But how the hell can you appreciate a woman who turns herself into Ernest Borgnine?

Tomorrow, while you're here screwing yourself into the floor, I'll be home with coffee and the comics and the "Today Show." And if I get an urge to exercise, I'll jog to the refrigerator and get a piece of leftover cheesecake. (*Beat.*) No, I've had it, I told you. So give it a rest here, okay? (*Beat.*) I don't care if there's still six months on my membership. I'll transfer it to the beanpole in the front row. Although I'm not sure I'd be doing her a favor. Another six months of bobbing up and down like a cork and she could disappear altogether.

ROBERTA

Achieving top status as a drummer in an all-male group is difficult.

Back in junior high I had a choice between the clarinet and the drums. To me, it wasn't much of a choice, you know. I mean, the clarinet it a ridiculous instrument. So I went for the drums. My mother freaked. She thought drums weren't feminine. But I persisted, and I got into the school band. I got the same reaction there. The guys didn't want to accept me as part of the drum section. But the instrument came easy for me, and in no time I was blowing them away. When my parents saw how I was a natural for the instrument, they bought me a used drum set and some warped cymbals. I spent hours practicing, I went wild for it, I loved it. I got into the great drummers, guys like Buddy Rich and Art Blakey and Tony Williams, and some of the rock players like Chad Smith and Mike Portnoy. I didn't have much formal training, because we didn't have an ace teacher here in my home town.

My first group experience was with an all-girl group called the Maidens. We weren't real together, but we were funky and we played a lot around the state. I didn't do a lot of fills. I just kept it in the pocket and concentrated on time. But I kept working on my technique and getting my chops together, trying to relax and let it flow. I watched a lot of videos and listened to a bunch of CDs.

Last April, I hear where The Plastic Dragon is looking for a drummer because their regular guy, Jimmy Wakeman, was moving to L.A. to do studio gigs. So, I figure, What the hell. They were going to be in Des Monies, so I drove up on a Sunday to where they were setting up for their show. I approached Rick Herman and asked if I could maybe try out for the job. He asked me about my experience, and I told him about the Maidens and the fact I'd won a state contest when I was in high school. He told me to come back for re-hearsals that afternoon.

At rehearsals, Jimmy Wakeman scared me to death. I almost walked out. He could do anything. It's like he was this octopus, you know. When he handed over the sticks, I was a mess, I had triple-shatters. And the other guys in the group weren't friendly. They all gave me The Ray. And being a chick, well . . . it was The Big Freeze, if you know what I mean.

For the first few bars I was pretty shaky until I fell into a groove with the bass player. Once I got in the pocket, I was okay, I relaxed, and everything fell into place. And playing with good musicians made it easier.

I've been with The Dragon ever since. And I get along with the guys real well. I guess they respect me because I can play. And, I mean, this is all that counts really. Sex has nothing to do with it. And besides, just because you're a guy doesn't mean you can swing.

ALICE

Nearly one quarter of American women now make more than their husbands. More money means more power—and new problems.

You're damned right I resent it. After all, who's the person bringing home the bacon? Just because you can't accept the fact I'm the breadwinner here, because you've still got this need to keep me in a housewifey position, I've got to come home after working ten hours and scrub out the toilet. The least you can do is pitch in and keep the house decent. Look at this. Shit all over the place. What the hell, did you get a Masters in sloppiness? C'mon, at least you can pick up after yourself. (*Beat.*) The recession my fault? Jesus, I'm going to get blamed for this, too? What the hell, we couldn't live on our savings forever. And you couldn't find anything, so I had to go to work.

Do you think I'm thrilled that I have to go to work every day while you change diapers and go to the park with Anna? It may be a great financial arrangement, but I'm miserable. I never thought of myself as a stay-at-home mother, but I hate being away from my daughter. To be perfectly honest, I wish to hell Anna were in day care. This way when I hold her, maybe she wouldn't cry for her daddy. How do you think this makes me feel? Shitty. Like I'm a totally inadequate mother.

(*Beat.*) Look, I like the job, but I'd quit in a minute. You think I wouldn't quit if you found something? I'd be out of there in a shot. But right now someone has to carry the load. (*Beat.*) Arrogant? What the hell's arrogant about the truth, for God's sake? This is reality. Your job hunting sure as hell didn't turn up anything. So what were we supposed to do in the meantime, go on welfare?

(*Beat.*) Hey, so you feel belittled, so what? Get over it. So what if I'm making more money than you ever did? You think you'd be happy. (*Beat.*) Frightening? Aw, c'mon. (*Beat.*) Okay, okay, I can understand. But look, this is a big adjustment for me, too. I mean, I have no problem with the *idea* of being the breadwinner. But sometimes the reality tears at me. And I know damned well it's starting to tear our marriage apart. But right now we can't afford for me to quit. We both know this.

(*Beat.*) Look, I know how you feel, I can sympathize. I know it's a blow to your self-esteem. But we've got to strike some kind of a balance here. We've got to adjust and face this as a team. I'm trying my best to juggle both worlds, but it isn't easy. And you're not making it any easier by crying about the fact I'm successful. What do you want me to be, a failure so your machismo won't be bruised?

Look, all I'm asking here is for a little understanding and for you to assume some of the household duties so I won't have to come home and clean out the johns at midnight.

JOSEY

Josey is the president of a multi-national media conglomerate. Here she berates a subordinate for thinking narrowly, and waxes maniacally regarding the power of the media.

Bizarre? Nothing's too bizarre today. Don't discount anything. Anything's possible, because the public will accept the impossible, because we've conditioned them for the incredible. If you entertain people, you can't lose, I don't give a damn how far out you go. We've proven it time and time again with our newspapers, our theme parks, our movies, television, magazines—you name it. Keep it simple and keep it emotional and don't try to pull any intellectual nonsense, because people are better than that. They want magic, illusion, adventure. They want fairy tales in color on big screens in stereo with big Dolby surround-sound. It's a supply-and-demand business. We create the demand, and we supply. A simple formula for wonderful people who came to this country because they were being suffocated by boredom. Not because of religious persecution—that's a crock of sentimental, church bullshit. They came because of boredom. How long can a person put up with sitting around on Saturday nights eating swill and committing incest and reading the Bible? They came over so they could have freedom of entertainment.

Every American has the inalienable right to entertainment. It's granted him. "Life, liberty, and the pursuit of happiness." *Happiness.* What do you think that means? It means entertainment. Like that first Thanksgiving. The Indians came and brought corn, right? Well, we're still bringing it, and people still love it because it's basic. It hits them where they live. Basic, solid, corny entertainment that makes 'em laugh and makes 'em cry and stirs 'em up. We've come a long way since the days of the pilgrims and a bunch of Indians dancing around half-naked to get laughs. Now, today, people have complete freedom from boredom. And why? Because of us, that's why. Because we understand them and love them and want the best for them. And the best is pure entertainment—electronic corn.

And remember—corn is American. Hell, the Indians knew it. Where do you think the word "media" comes from? From the word "mead." Mead—media. And the best media is bright and colorful and loud and immediate and unreal. If I'd been content to sit back and keep doing the "real" news and "real" movies and "real" television, where the do you think people would be today? In libraries loading their lungs with the dust of antiquity. At dramas listening to "lofty" bullshit about the plight of the masses. At concerts where not one goddamned instrument is amplified. Why hell, people would be back to incest and the Bible—bored shitless. I realized a long time ago that my destiny, my responsibility, my duty as an American, was to preserve life, liberty and, the pursuit of happiness.

Happiness. That's what liberty is all about. What's the point of freedom if you're not happy? People deserve to be happy, and by God they're going to be—whether they like it or not.

DANA

Some days, no matter what you do, you look and feel like hell.

You get up in the morning. You look in the mirror. Eek! This is me? It can't be me. It's something from another planet. You can't believe it. You're ugly. That's not hair, that's a ball of yarn full of snot. You can smell your own breath. It knocks you over. You don't know whether to brush your teeth or call in a plumber. You squint but you can't focus because your eyes are stuck shut at the corners. You look older. In just eight hours you've aged twenty years. Yesterday you were at least semi-attractive. Today . . . you know the feeling, I don't have to tell you.

You take a shower and drop the soap on your toe with the corn. You get out of the shower and look in the mirror and you're still ugly. Only difference is, now you're ugly and wet. You try to dry off the ugly, but it sticks. You blow-dry the snot out of your hair and it becomes the consistency of a beard. You go to your closet and stand there nude, looking into your clothes. They all look like Goodwill. The clothes look back. You close your eyes and grab something. Clothes roulette. You pull on pantyhose and they don't have feet. You dig out the best pair. The one with only three runs. You say "fuck" three times. You know the feeling, I don't have to tell you.

You squeeze into the dress. You reach around to zip up the back and aggravate your tennis elbow. You check yourself out. You look like you're wearing another person. You try to smooth out the bumps but you can't because the bumps are on you. You pull at the dress but there's no give because the goddamn thing fits like a wetsuit. You'd change, but you can't stand the thought of another look in your closet. You still look ugly, but now you're ugly and uncomfortable.

You try to do something with your hair. A brush and comb won't get it. You need power tools. You kind of arrange it, and waste a can of hairspray on it. God. It looks like you've got muskrats fighting on your head. There's no getting around it, this is going to be a bad hair day. You know the feeling, I don't have to tell you.

You make a stab at lipstick. You dig around in a drawer full of crap and choose Crimson Desire, which goes on like Red Vomit. Then makeup. L'Oréal's Matte Finish turns your face into a buckwheat pancake. The mascara's gummy and you wind up with caterpillars on your lashes. By now your eyes are unstuck, which is a mixed blessing because you can see that you look like a mime. You're a general mess. You'd start all over, but you haven't got time. You've got to be in the office in forty minutes, which is forty-five minutes away which means you've got to drive seventy miles an hour while drinking coffee in heavy traffic. Besides, what's the point. You could do it all over and it wouldn't make any difference. Somedays, no matter what you do, you're still gonna look like shit. You know the feeling, I don't have to tell you.

JANIS

*Her kitchen is a mess. Her hair is in curlers. She's wearing an old
house dress. But Janis doesn't have time for appearances, she's
engaged in the serious occupation of keeping an eye on the neighborhood. In this scene, she is speaking on a cordless phone to Doris,
her friend, neighbor, and fellow neighborhood watchdog.*

I seen him, Doris. Came in around midnight. Twelve thirteen, to be
exact. He ain't working this late, baby, no way. 'Less the post office
is runnin' overtime. Then the screamin' and yellin' started in.
Whoooee! Then the crashin' and bangin' . . . No, who could blame
her. He was my husband, I'd snip that sucker off . . . Oh, I didn't
know that . . . Is that right? Whoooee! Maybe we can get him to pass
that big thing around. Maybe we can get that crazy mailman to make
a couple deliveries in our slot—know that I mean. (*She chuckles.*)
You hear about Esther? . . . She went and had that liposuction on her
butt . . . That's right. They sucked about twenty pounds of butt off
that girl. You seen her? . . . Well, you ain't gonna recognize her
without that roast beef in her pants. I dunno, though. I don't want
them people sticking that thing in my body. Don't know what they're
liable to do. What if they get in too deep and suck out you liver? . . .
Yeah, me too . . . No! You sure? Billie White and her husband
swingers? Billie White? This can't be, girl. Billie White don't know
anything about sex . . . Crotchless panties? Naw, can't be . . . Leather
garter belt? . . . Naw. You sure? She showed 'em to you? Why
would she wanna go do something like that? . . . Videotapes! Don't
tell me about it. The thought of all them people tied up in sweaty
knots is *disgusting*!

Guess who I seen at the beauty parlor yesterday? Lena James.
Lookin' bad . . . She got one of them hairdos where they shave up the
sides and leave the top long and spiky . . . A woman that age should

know better. Besides, what good will it do—she's still gonna be a hundred and fifty pounds of ugly . . . He did? I'll be double-upside-down-damn. I guess you just can't ever tell anymore these days . . . Well, it don't happen overnight. He probably played with Ken dolls when he was a kid . . . Poor Ruthie. I mean, it's gotta be real unsettling to find out you're husband's . . . Oh, well, live and let live, I always say . . . Did I tell you that Darla and Jim lost their house? . . . Bank took it back. This is what happens when you live high. Their whole life was on credit cards. She even paid for her hysterectomy with Master Card. That eighteen percent eats a person alive.

What? . . . Please, don't tell me, I don't wanna hear it. Are you sure? No! Holy shit! Well, this is what happens when you spend eight hours a day on your back. You was bound to get caught sooner or later. I kept telling you, girl, I kept telling you, what did I tell you? How you gonna explain this to Ralph; he's had a vasectomy? . . . Why, this'll kill 'im. And then—he'll kill you. You're in big trouble, girl. Damn . . . Me say anything? Are you kidding? You know me. I didn't hear anything. Doris who? I never met you, you're a total stranger . . . Okay. Call me if you need help. I'll come on over, whatever. Bye, doll. (*She kills the conversation, then quickly dials another number.*) Hello, Lena . . . Now don't you repeat a word of this girl, you understand? But guess what happened to old Motel Butt . . .

DR. MARABELL SMITH

Dr. Smith is a no-nonsense psychotherapist in a small Midwestern town. Her methods are direct, unorthodox, and effective. She is a larger-than-life person, and a true eccentric. She leans back in her rickety swivel-chair casually, gives her mouth a liberal spritz of Binaca, and begins to proselytize in her energetic, effusive manner.

Okay, so what's your problem? (*Beat.*) Depression? That's obvious. You have the melancholy air of depression in your eyes. (*Beat.*) And you contemplate suicide. Well, how are you going to do it? Gun, rope, pills, poison, leaping, drowning—carbon monoxide? Or do you have some exotic plan for self-extinction? I had one patient, a woman from Muncie with sexual ambiguities, who was going to smother herself in a tub of Chanel. Very imaginative, but I'm afraid the costs were prohibitive. I saw her maybe six, seven times. Nice person. She's alive and well and living in Seattle now with another lesbian. I get a card from her every year on Gertrude Stein's birthday.

(*Beat.*) You thought I'd want to prevent you from killing yourself? Whatever gave you a crazy idea like that? (*Beat.*) Because it's general practice? The hell with general practice. What's so marvelous about general practice? About Freud, and Jung, and Adler, and a half dozen other guys who were more involved with proving their own theories than the milk of human kindness? What ever happened to common-sense values, to chivalry? Ever since the twenties and thirties, when Nietzscheanism and Freudianism got a foothold and became major intellectual and moral influences, we've become saturated with guiltlessness. Today, anything goes because the psychoanalytic society says, "Hey, do your own thing," even if doing your own thing means being a rude bastard or pushing your crippled granny off a rooftop.

I'm not here to save lives. I'm not some psychological lifeguard. I'm not a hand-holder and cajoler and I don't show ink blots and do tests and talk about your mother. Because all of that is irrelevant. I'm not about to "put you in touch with your feelings." Frankly, I don't give a bloody damn about your feelings. All I want to do is—to use an automotive analogy—fix you so you run right. And we do this by looking at the facts instead of a bunch of arcane little splotches, and delving into potty training. Look, if you want someone like that, there are plenty of 'em in the Yellow Pages listed under Mixed Nuts. If you want to involve yourself with interminable, painstaking intro-spection to the tune of your entire savings, these are the boys for you. On the other hand, if you want to get out from under the layer of mental cheesecloth without frills and foolishness, stick it out here with me for a few sessions. And if you want to jump nude into the Maumee River at high noon, be my guest, okay? That's the first thing you've got to realize. That I don't give a good doodly-damn about your suicidal tendencies.

MARIA

As an enlisted sailor, she has spent her first seven years overseas, an experience that has opened her eyes to the untoward realities of military behavior. Here she confronts a macho lieutenant regarding his attitude, and the attitude of many of his ilk, with respect to women.

I'm *not* being totally negative. I just can't overlook facts, that's all. (*Beat.*) Yes, that's right—facts. I suppose you think Tailhook didn't happen? (*Beat.*) Like hell they were set up. They got caught, and they got what was coming to them. They were a bunch of drunked-up, out-of-control assholes who thought they could get away with it because this has been the drill for years. (*Beat.*) C'mon, face it, women are nothing but sex objects to these creeps. I think it's about time someone blew the whistle. It took a lot of courage. If I'd been in her shoes, I don't know if I could have hung in there. I have a lot of respect for her. (*Beat.*) A troublemaker? It figures this would be your attitude. She had it coming, right? (*Beat.*) Yeah, sure. Like women who get raped, they ask for it. You ignorant sonofabitch.

(*Beat.*) Oh, you don't like my language, huh? I'm sure you've never heard it before. Hell, half of the words that come out of your mouth are garbage. Especially when women are around. You do it either to embarrass us or to show us what a big man you are. Hey, if you were so damned big, you wouldn't have to use profanity to order a cup of coffee.

(*Beat.*) Don't lay that crap on me, mister. You're talking to someone who spent seven years overseas in the Philippines and Korea. I know how our "boys in uniform" behave. The only thing half-way accurate about that phrase is the word "boys." I've lived with 'em. I've seen 'em in action, and I don't mean in battle. What a load of crud. (*Beat.*) Yes, crud! So far as I'm concerned, ninety-five percent of military men are scum. (*Beat.*) Oh, I'm being unfair.

Sorry, I take it back. Ninety percent. This leaves us with a whopping ten percent who aren't toilet scrapings. (*Beat.*) Oh, a bitch, huh? This is your intellectual response? Okay, I admit it—I'm a bitch. And I'm going to continue to be a bitch until men like you stop treating women like vaginas on wheels.

How do you think I got to be this way? (*Beat.*) No, I wasn't born with an attitude. When I came into the Navy, I came in with an open mind, no preconceived ideas. But after seven years overseas, that's all changed. And why? Because I've seen married officers take girls as young as nine and share them with the whole crew. "Old enough to bleed, old enough to breed" is what the guys used to say. Lovely, huh? The guys in my unit would sit around and crack jokes about how they had faithful wives back home while they were making it with kids and hookers. Hell, maybe I do have an attitude. If I do, it's justified. (*Beat.*) You were overseas, and you didn't fool around. Yeah, sure and I'm Admiral Nimitz. The way you treat women? If I ever run into your wife, I'm going to give her some good advice. I'm going to tell her to get an HIV test—*fast.*

TRACY

At extremely liberal Antioch College, they have imposed rules to be observed by sexually active students. Sexual partners are expected to explicitly verbalize their sexual intentions—"May I touch your breast" for example. Well, this is a bit much for Tracy. She views this as PC gone rampant.

Fucking Antioch has always been ridiculous. Since, like, forever. I used to live in Springfield, Ohio, and when I was a teenager we used to go down there and get loaded on Argentinean beer. At a place called the Old Trail Tavern. Awesome burgers. It's a neat little town. Beautiful, actually. Except it's always been Ohio's Moscow. And now it's, like, so "in" you can't afford to live there because a bunch of rich people who hate America because you can get rich here have taken over the place with big houses and Range Rovers. And these people are beyond liberal, they're fucking Mao up to their fannypacks. I had a bet with a friend that more McGovern bumper stickers were sold in Yellow Springs than anywhere else on the planet.

I remember how we used to break up at how serious the students took themselves. Always looked like they were constipated with intellect, you know. Lots of little rich girls in Goodwill sweaters and sandals. Never wore makeup because it would be worldly, you know. Or worse than worldly—they might even stumble into being attractive. Heaven forbid you look good. Then there were the guys with the bad-fitting corduroy jackets and stringy hair and straggly beards. And everyone seemed to have the complexion of wet newspaper. They looked like a bunch of refugees from Bleak House.

The sexual-rules thing is typical of the place. Who the hell is surprised? As if at Antioch sex is something they've just discovered. The guys from Springfield used to go down there because they knew it was easier to lay a free-love Commie than masturbate. The chicks in this town weren't just easy, they were mousey-looking little Kierkegaard freaks who'd fuck a woodpile if there was a snake in it. So the middle-class guys from Springfield would go down there and binge on liberal college pussy.

And now they've got Sexual Rules. Whooo! Wow! Sexual *Rules*. Like, "May I touch your tit?" "Mind if I fondle your nipple?" You've got to be super-specific. This way you get permission, and you can't offend anyone or violate the sanctity of their private parts or screw up their delicate little psyches. Because now there are Sexual Rules.

Hey, why not? After all, this *is* Antioch. And I think it's neat. It keeps the off-the-wall tradition of the place intact. I love it. Because when I go back home, I know I can go to Yellow Springs and it'll be exactly the same, like always; wacky and bohemian and fringe-Commie. Some things, even though you know they're wacko, you love because there's this sense of security in knowing that you can depend on them being fucked up.

LYNN

Her mother is an embarrassment. She dresses like a hooker, she attempts to remain a perennial teenager. Here Lynn lays it on the line.

Look, Mom, it's getting to the point where I don't want to bring anyone over here anymore. (*Beat.*) Yeah, this *is* the way I feel. Can you blame me? I mean, after all—look at you. What kind of outfit do you call this? You part of a clown act here, or something? For fuck's sake, you look like Bozo. (*Beat.*) I know it's no way to talk to you, but what do you expect? I've tried to be subtle. I've intimated, I've hinted, I've questioned. Like the mini-skirt you wore to Sandy's wedding. I tried to discourage it. But you had to wear it and make a goddamn fool of yourself and embarrass the hell outta me in the process. (*Beat.*) Yes, I *was* ashamed. Don't you think I should have been? (*Beat.*) No, I guess you wouldn't because you just don't get it. A woman your age doesn't wear something like that—anytime. It was ridiculous. Every time you crossed your legs, half the men in the place damned near fell off their chairs. Even the minister, he kept losing his place in the sermon from staring at your crotch. (*Beat.*) C'mon, no way. Fashion, bullshit. It's your way of calling attention to yourself because you can't stand the thought of getting old. (*Beat.*) Like hell. I'm not buying.

I can't blame Dad for leaving. How long could he put up with being married to Miss Teen America? And look who he remarried. A woman almost ten years older. This doesn't tell you something? (*Beat.*) Nonsense, he traded you in for maturity, for a woman he could relate to, for someone he could be comfortable with.

Do you have any idea how silly you look? (*Beat.*) I don't give a damn. Your feelings get hurt, they get hurt. Somebody has to tell you before you succeed in making a total jerk of yourself. Before you go for another face-lift. Hell, you already look like waxed fruit. And the way you talk, trying to be "today" or "hip" or what-the-hell-ever, what the hell's *this* all about? You should hear yourself. And this, this wardrobe, this . . . whatever the fuck you call it? And what's with the haircut? You trying to look like Moe Howard? And the eye shadow, and the black lipstick, and the . . . Christ, you look like a five-dollar hooker. (*Beat.*) So I'm a little bitch. I'd rather be a little bitch than an old fool. (*Beat.*) Okay, I'll get out, I'm going. But you'd better give some serious thought to what I'm saying here. You'd better wake up and face up to your age and quit trying to come on like you're a member of a rap group. Because if you don't, you're gonna wind up alone because nobody is going to associate with an old woman who looks like something the dog dug up during an Easter egg hunt.

GEENA

She gives a locksmith some background leading to her decision to change the lock on her door.

Here we are, in bed. I'm reading a good book. So I say, "Not tonight." You'd think I'd said, "Not ever." He gets pissed. He rolls over like some kid, you know. Next morning, he's still uptight. I tell him to chill out and he goes into a thing. I listen. When he's finished, he slams out of the place like a fool.

He comes home last night like nothing ever happened. Like he never said I was a cold bitch, like that morning he wasn't Mr. Fred Asshole USA. It's, like, now everything's supposed to be cool because he's decided to be a real big man and forget it, right? And I'm supposed to forget all about him acting like Mr. Turd All American. Well, this isn't the the way it works. I go, "You mean to tell me that after treating me like shit this morning that now it's all forgotten because you've decided to give me a break, right? Well, Mr. Dickhead Universe, this ain't gonna be the case, okay?"

He looks at me real funny. He's offended. He gets on his hound-dog look. I just broke his heart. He's offended that I ain't gonna forgive *him* for calling *me* names and slamming the door so hard he knocked stuff off the mantle. He can't get behind this. It's too deep for him. You can see it in his eyes. They're glassed over more than usual. He goes, "Some damned book you were reading was more important than me. And I was horny."

I say, "Babe, every time you're horny I don't automatically turn on like a microwave. What I got down here ain't no major appliance."

He goes, "Yeah, but. . . . " He goes, "Yeah, but" a lot when he's over his head because after "Yeah, but" there ain't ever anything else he can think of to say. So before he gets off another "Yeah, but," I tell him, "Honey, when I'm not feelin' hot/You can keep what you got. And last night the last thing I wanted to do was get involved with the little thing between your legs." Whooee. This was shot low and direct, and it hit him where the flowers grow. He didn't know whether to puke or go blind. He just stammers and gets all red and his cheeks puff out like he's got an air hose up his sarcastic little butt.

He goes, "That's a hell of a thing to say."

I go, "But what you say is okay, huh? You can be Mr. Joe B. Bastard and it's okay, right? You can be an asshole, and chew me up and down, and slam doors, and this is cool, huh, Mr. Pencilpeter?"

"Don't you go calling me that," he says. "You ain't ever had any complaints before."

I say, "Yeah, that's because my mamma always told me to be thankful for the little things in life." Now he gets even redder. It's like he's gonna bust and blow all over the room.

He says, " I don't have to take this shit. I don't need your insults. What's your claim to fame, bitch?"

I tell him, "My claim to fame is that I'm the world's best at faking orgasims." He goes nuts and calls me . . . you name it. Then he goes and slams out the door. Prick.

Maybe you better put on a deadbolt, too.

ROSE

It is often difficult when your family backgrounds are really different. And Rose Shapiro knows just how difficult it can be. Born in Shaker Heights, Ohio, of an Orthodox Jewish family, she has confronted a true dilemma in adjusting to her husband's West Virginia relations.

Frank's family is really Waspy. They look like they materialized right off a sampler. Nice people, but boy are they ever straight. The women all have these tight little hairdos and wear cardigan sweaters and clunky shoes. And the men are very big on Banlon. Frank calls his Uncle Harry "The Prince of Polyester." They live in Bluefield, West Virginia. We visit them during the holidays, and we usually spend a week there during the summer. It's a beautiful place—isolated but lovely. But this is really WASP City. I mean, when I'm there, I represent the resident Jew.

The first time Frank took me home, I think the whole bunch kind of went into shock. When I told them my name was Shapiro, there was, like, this silence you could hear all the way to Boston. They just kind of stood there riveted like they'd been sprayed with Krazy Glue. It was a real trip. Here I was, this outspoken Jewish girl wearing dramatic clothing, and bright red lipstick, in the middle of a Grange meeting. For the first time in my life I felt really *ethnic*. Frank made some awkward introductions and everyone was very polite, but you could feel, like, this embarrassed tension, you know. Like when someone breaks wind in a large gathering. Creepy.

We were going to tell them that we planned on getting married, but we decided to wait a couple of days, to let the reality of me being Jewish sink in. I think if we'd sprung it on them immediately there would have been a group stroke. So we decided to cool it.

The whole scene was spooky. I felt awkward and out of sync. And I found myself trying to act "normal." Weird. Frank's dad made an effort to be casual about the whole thing, but he just succeeded in making a fool of himself. He'd say things like, "I had a Jew doctor once. They make good doctors." Then he'd try to lighten things up with these terrible jokes that were about as funny as hemorrhoids. He asked me if I played the Jewish piano. I didn't have a clue as to what he was talking about. "You know, the Jewish piano," he said, "the cash register."

We've been married for about two years now. Living in Cleveland, thank God. Frank's working for my father in the insurance business. His family's been up only once. What a disaster. When we did Seder, they reacted as though we were into some bizarre rite, or something. Later, Frank's dad remarked that our yarmulkes made us look like monkeys. This was supposed to be funny. I thought my brother was going to run a halavah through his heart. Of course, my family took some pretty cheap shots at West Virgina, too. You know, the Moonshine State, the barefoot-and-pregnant thing—all of that garbage.

Seeing the two families together made me realize how far apart some people are. But, what the hell, in spite of it, we're getting along. And that's the important thing—getting along.

CHRISTINA

Christina is David's second wife, but in the eyes of David's mother, she can't measure up to his first wife, Diane. She dearly loved Diane, found her flawless in every respect, and throws her up to Christina at every opportunity. Christina has finally had it with the carping and criticizing and in this scene vents in no uncertain terms.

All right, okay! That's it! I've had it! If you don't like tuna casserole, don't eat the goddamn thing. It's the best I can do after working for eight hours, okay? And frankly, I don't give a shit if Diane was a gourmet cook or not. Good for Diane. She had time to fuck around with watercress all day because she was a lazy bitch who leaned on David, and sucked him dry, and left him with $35,000 worth of credit-card debt. In spite of what you think, Diane wasn't Mother Theresa, Eleanor Roosevelt, Madame Curie, and Jackie Onasis rolled into one, big, perfect package. She was a self-centered user who didn't give a damn for your son. Thank God they didn't have children.

And that's another thing. I'm sick and tired of you criticizing me for the way I'm raising Kelly. I didn't appreciate the remark that she looks like refugee. I buy her oversize clothing so they'll last longer, because we have to conserve because we're struggling to pay off Master Card at eighteen percent because of sweet, wonderful Diane. And the next time Kelly's not feeling well, don't you ever suggest that I give her an enema. What the hell is this, the Middle Ages? If anyone around here needs a good cleaning out, it's you. Just stay the hell out of the way I raise my child.

And I'm not putting up with you taking any more calls from Diane. Look, I know you think she's the greatest thing since Microsoft, but don't you realize it hurts me when you talk to her with me here? Or is this planned? Sometimes I get the distinct impression that it's your intention to go out of the way to see how shitty you can be.

I can't be everything to everybody, I can only be me, and David and I can only be us. I'm not a saint, and don't pretend to be, and anyone who does, like Diane d'Arc, is standing in a pile of it up to her nose. I realize that I'm nothing like her. I work—she didn't; I don't go to church—she did; I'm considerate of David—she wasn't. Look, if Diane is so wonderful, why isn't David still married to her? Have you ever taken time to run this past your narrow perspective? Diane's a turkey, that's why. She's a complainer, a phony, a testimony to Home Shopping. She's a *loser*.

So let's get this straight once and for all. If you're going to live here, you can either accept my way of doing things or you can move out. I'll help you pack. Then we'll call Diane and tell her you've decided to move in with her. Then we'll see how much she loves you. Wanna make a little bet? I'll bet you this house against your shoes that alluva sudden she's decided to move to Detroit.

JANET

Her daughter had always been an anomaly. But to Janet, this is what differentiates her from the pack, makes her a unique human being.

She was always . . . different. Even as a kid. Never like the others. Used to spend a lot of time alone. Could have been because her father walked out. Who knows? Or maybe it was because she was always big for her age. At first she had trouble with school, couldn't seem to find herself. She didn't have many friends that I can remember, just one boy down the block who used to come home with her every now and then after school. Like I said, she was different.

She was a good daughter. Never any trouble. Liked to hang around the house. Never had to worry about her getting into gangs, or doing drugs, anything like that. And we got along good. She helped out around the house and was always understanding when the money was low. She was a good kid. But . . . different, like I said.

I used to notice how she wasn't like . . . average. Didn't like dolls, girls' games, the usual stuff you'd expect. But, so? Besides, like I mentioned, she was a good kid and never gave me any trouble. Then in junior high, she alluva sudden got interested in sports. And this seemed to change her, and she opened up and became more outgoing. She was on the track team and played softball. And she was outstanding. I used to go watch her and was amazed. I never had any talent for sports. No one in the family did that I can remember.

In high school she was on the varsity volleyball team and led them to the state finals. She wiped everybody. Could leap like a kangaroo, and could spike the ball so hard nobody could return it. Amazing, really amazing. And as a kid she's been so passive. Who knows?

She got into Michigan State on a volleyball scholarship. She was outstanding there, too. Got written up in all the major newspapers, even *Sports Illustrated*. She had it, natural talent, you know. She majored in education with an eye on coaching.

Little by little I heard less and less from her. She was into her studies and her volleyball thing and had friends and—like it always seems to happen—she just kind of grew away from home.

After college she moved New York state where she's a phys-ed teacher at high school in Elmira. I see her maybe, two, three times a year. Last Christmas she brought a friend home, a nice girl named Brandy, a teacher at her school. It was good having them around. Before she left she told me about them. Not that I was surprised. I had a feeling.

She said the decision had been hard for her. I mean, sorting things out, making a commitment and all. And then there was the potential problems at school: parents, the school board, and the like. It was a big step. So far, so good. Everything's going okay.

She asked if I understood. It was hard for her, I could tell. Why wouldn't I understand? I mean, what's to understand? I told her it didn't change anything. I told her she'd always been different, and that her difference made her a special person. I told her I love her. I told her that nobody could hope for a better daughter.

RUTHIE

A feeling person, an animal lover, Ruthie is committed to alternative medicine in the treatment of her ailing pet.

All right, so I'm an animal nut. Okay, I admit it. I love animals. I've always loved animals, all creatures great, small, medium, short, tall, and extra large—all sizes. (*Beat.*) Look, it's just me, that's all. I was born an animal person. Maybe it has to do with the fact I was raised on a farm, I don't know. Even as a kid I had every kind of pet imaginable: hamsters, cats, dogs, snakes—you name it. And I couldn't stand the thought of an animal being mistreated. I hated it when they butchered. I used to cry and couldn't sleep and I got sick. (*Beat.*) I know, I know that. I know it's part of farm life. That's what my mother and father tried to explain to me. But it didn't work. One time before they butchered, I let all the pigs out. I thought I was saving them. They ran all over the farm. Took them a day to round them up. Boy, did I ever catch hell for that.

(*Beat.*) It's got nothing to do with being politically correct. I don't know anything about that. Besides, what the hell do animals have to do with politics? Even though most of the people in office are lying pigs. It's got to do with common sense. I mean, who in their right mind wants to hurt an animal? Who wants to see a helpless creature suffer? Nobody, unless they're some kind of fucking sicko. That's the reason we've got to do whatever we can. Least ways, I do. So, regardless of what you think, I'm taking Pepper to an acupuncturist.

(*Beat.*) It's not stupid. Why is it stupid? Because you say so? Hey, there's a lot more to healing than medicine and surgery. And this goes for humans as well as animals. Why in hell is that the first thing most doctors want to do is start cutting? Like your mother. She should have never been opened up. (*Beat.*) I'm not blaming you. Stop being so defensive. What I'm saying is, there are other methods, other treatments that can be tried before they start hacking. Who the hell knows about the mysteries of healing? This is the reason we've got to give alternative medicine a chance.

(*Beat.*) Look, we've been over this a thousand times. I'm not putting Pepper to sleep without a fight. And the other vets with their conventional methods can go take a fucking leap, because I'm trying acupuncture. I'm taking Pepper to Dr. Rabin this morning, and frankly, I don't care what you, or Dr. Adams, or your sister, or God think! (*Beat.*) Well then . . . you'll just have to be pissed, won't you? You'll have to get over it—or you won't. I know one thing, if I go along with you and that muscle-head Adams, Pepper will be dead meat by noon. Adams, like too damned many others, because he's locked in his little crucible of academia, isn't open to new approaches. I'm not caving in to his "logic."

I've watched Adams with animals. He handles them like they're sacks of flour, something lifeless and unfeeling. This heavy-handed, cut-and-dried sonofabitch shouldn't be practicing. Because he hasn't got a clue to the fact that love is the only force that can make us sensitive and responsive to the needs of others. Animals *and* people.

JANE

It's difficult to know a person's true history. There are certain re-lationships into which you enter without trepidation and suspicion. Especially those involving love.

You don't know. How can you, really? Do you go back into personal records like the CIA? Love just doesn't work like that. When you're up to your neck in desire and caring, you don't question, you just savor the moments and look forward.

We met in a library in North Hollywood. He was reading Faulkner and I was there gathering information on a piece I was doing on the music industry; about payola and the influence of drugs in the industry. It was a nightmare. I had stuff strewn all over the table we were sharing. I couldn't seem to pull anything together. I was totally blanked. Well, Robert noticed the articles and apparently sensed that I was about to explode. He asked if he could be of help. It turns out that he'd been in the record business. It was, like, he'd been dropped in from heaven. He filled me in about the business, chronology, a bunch of critical details. He was very articulate and informative. Saved my ass.

Robert was a free-lance screenwriter with a couple of reasonable credits. He was intelligent and extremely literary. And he had a great sense of humor. Right away the vibes were right. I mean, we're both writers, about the same age, similar backgrounds. And as an added plus, he was attractive. So . . . do I have to tell you?

Robert moved into my place in West Hollywood. He didn't come with much stuff. Just a few pieces of clothing, a lot of books, and an old Mac Classic II. This was basically it. This is one of the things I liked about him, that he was so uncluttered and unencumbered, not ruled by possessions. He was a person who wasn't loaded down with a pile of yesterday's garbage.

Our relationship was fabulous. We had so much in common. And day after day I fell more in more in love with the man. It was an easy, give-and-take situation, without any of the usual childish possessiveness and stupid mind games. He was the first man I'd ever met who didn't have an ounce of jealously. It was refreshing. He had his thing—I had mine.

The first symptom was this hacking cough. It just got worse and worse. I figured a cold, right? Maybe a touch of bronchitis. But it became more severe. Finally he went to a doctor.

I'll never forget the afternoon he told me. God, I was devastated. Not only for him, but for the lie, for him not being open up front about being bi. I can't tell you what I went through at that moment. I was shattered, frustrated, I was . . . I was goddamned mad! I loved him so damned much, and now, I mean . . . shit! And then there was the fear.

I saw my doctor the next morning. Thank God, I was negative. But Robert. . . . It was the inevitable downhill slide. We were together till the end. In spite of everything, I still loved him. It was a terrible year, but in many ways it was beautiful. Even though he was degenerating rapidly, he seemed to burn brightly during that time, like his sickness lit up inside. His mind and his wit were more acute than ever. And he never complained. He was courageous till . . . well . . . till it was over.

Looking back, I wouldn't have done anything different. My time with Robert was special. He was a hell of a guy.

LAURA

The glamour of the land of the Rich and Famous is in the eye of the beholder.

I don't know anything about mountains. I'm a Vegas Strip person myself. But it sounded cool. Aspen. I mean, Jesus, this is where the rich and the famous go to crack their femurs. I couldn't wait. I say, "Honey, load up the Caddy and let's boogie." Or something to that effect.

We drive to Colorado. It's something else. Like, blue skies with puffy clouds, snow-capped mountains, and green valleys. This is a state. This is a picture. I can understand why John Denver sings high-pitched songs about it.

We check into the Little Nell. A great hotel next to the ski lifts. The room is something. A wall-to-wall bed, a sauna, a fireplace, and a view of Aspen Mountain. Eight hundred a night. Expensive. But, what the hell, Harry's been lucky at Keno.

Harry says we gotta hit the slopes. I'm not thrilled, but what the fuck? So we go rent ski equipment. They put me into a suit of many colors and I zip up and look like a purple and chartreuse stuffed-sausage. Then I get these clunky boots and skis. They send me to the bunny slope, where there's no rabbits, just people falling down and screaming. Nightmare. Harry goes off while I get instructions from a guy named Heinz. Blonde, blue eyes with a Nazi accent. He says I got natural athletic ability. I say he's full of bullshit because I can't even watch TV bowling without getting aches and pains. After a half hour my legs feel like they aren't hooked onto my body. Screw this. I go back to the room and soak in the sauna and Harry comes in with a face as red as a baboon's butt. He says it's healthy out on the slopes, and I tell him I'll take a smoke-filled room at the Desert Inn.

We get dressed and go to party of high-rollers at a glass house up in the mountains. Friends of Harry's gambling buddy Waxy Irving, so called because he's so slick at 21. Waxy is talking to John Denver, whose real name turns out to be Deutschendorf. Deutschendorf, Heinz—I figure with names like this, Hitler could be hiding out in Snowmass. You never know.

The women are tall and weigh three pounds. Very tanned with big-time face-lifts. And not very swift. When I ask one if she ever saw *The Midnight Idol*, she thinks I'm talking about Tom Snyder. People who haven't heard of Wayne Newton have got to be from another planet.

We have a sit-down dinner. They serve wild game. Venison. I eat the peas. After dinner this oom-pah band in leather pants plays "old-world favorites" and yodels. More German stuff. Then Martina Navratilova shows up. Nazis and Commies. What the fuck? I tell Harry to make excuses, that I'm dying with all this foreign shit and nothing but peas in my stomach.

Next morning, I'm outta there. Harry's pissed, but so what? I'm not about to spend another day falling down in the snow with Heinz. So we split back to Vegas.

I sure was great to get back among normal people.

CARRIE

Maintaining propriety at all costs is a psychological illness that ultimately results in disastrous consequences.

Yes, Mother, it was a beautiful funeral. (*Beat.*) Yes. Yes. (*Beat.*) No, I didn't notice. Frankly, I don't care *what* Janet was wearing. (*Beat.*) For Christ's sake, Mother, who cares? (*Beat.*) Will you please stop it? Do you realize what you're saying? You'd think you'd be touched by the fact that she and Jim drove all the way up here from Louisville to be with you. Instead, you're bitching because she wore the wrong dress. Whatever the "wrong" dress is. Is there some fundamental costume that you wear to a funeral? (*Beat.*) No, I don't agree. And I think this conversation is superficial. (*Beat.*) Respect? Respect for what? You'd think, after what you two have been through, you'd be thrilled that she even showed up. Instead, you've got to bitch that she wasn't presentable. (*Beat.*) Mother . . . Mother. Mother, will you please shut up about it? Good Lord.

It's the same old same old, isn't it? Just like always. Appearances. How things "look." What will people "think." At a time like this, who gives a damn what they—who-the-hell-ever "they" are—what anybody thinks? Do you realize what you said to me when you called to tell me Dad killed himself? (*Beat.*) How else do you want me to put it? This is what happened, isn't it? The man committed suicide. (*Beat.*) Awkward? I don't believe this. Awkward for whom? (*Beat.*) Bullshit! All you're concerned with here is how Dad's taking his own life will reflect on you. Just like you were embarrassed because Janet didn't look like Princess Di. And how about what you said to me. "Do you still have that awful haircut?" What the hell kind of remark was this on top of the news that my father had blown the top of his head off? Here I was, in total shock, mind-numbed, and the next words out of your mouth was some stupid drivel about my hairstyle.

(*Beat.*) You didn't mean anything by it. *Of course* you meant something by it. Why the hell else would you have brought it up at a time like this?

And you wonder why Janet hasn't spoken to you in over five years. Your own daughter. (*Beat.*) She's *not* unreasonable. No way. I'm not buying into this. All she wants is to be left alone to live her own life, that's all. You and your damned controlling, judgmental attitude, no wonder you lost her. You don't approve of Jim, you think her kids should be in private schools, they spend too much money on "silliness." What the fuck's it to you—it's their money.

(*Beat.*) All right, all right. I'm sorry if I've upset you. I apologize. And I know you loved Dad, and that you've got to be going though hell. And I'm here, and I'll stay around as long as you want. But, Mom, you got to stop putting appearances over what's really important. You've always done this. And it's sick, don't you realize? Sick! So, for your own good, I've got to lay in on you cold right now. Look, Dad killed himself. Tragic, but this is reality. And we're not going to pretend any differently, okay? For once in your life, I beg you, put the truth over appearances and how things reflect on you. And please, go downstairs right now and make up with Janet. Start being a mother instead of self-consumed pain.

PAULA

She is a strong woman, self-reliant and successful in the business world. She doesn't need, and won't tolerate, a controlling man.

I don't do laundry, I don't do shirts, I don't fold clothes, I don't do dishes, I don't dust, I don't cook, I don't vacuum, I don't schlep groceries, I don't make beds, I don't take out trash, I don't water plants, I don't wash windows, I don't flounce curtains. I don't do any of this. I pay a person to come in and wrestle with this stuff, because I make $86,000 a year working my ass off ten hours a day selling software to guys who resent the fact that I pick up their lunch tabs.

And I resent you moving in here and expecting me to be Little Miss Muffett. If you don't like the arrangement, let's unarrange it right now, okay? Because I'm never going to be Betty Crocker. I don't give a damn about rinse cycles and Hefty Bags and curtain rods and Revere Wear and Clorox and major appliances and the fact that Ivory soap floats. This is for people like my mother who was a slave to my father who sat in a chair and burped Budweiser while she painted the house.

You're in the wrong picture here, pal. You've got a bit part in *Dick and Jane Play House* while I'm starring in *Jane Doesn't Take Dick's Shit*. I don't know where you've been, but just in case you haven't heard, women are actually mastering the ABCs. Are you a fucking Neanderthal, or something, Fred Flintstone in Armani suits? Look, you're a nice-looking guy and good in bed. But looks and sex don't qualify you to come in here and start dictating. In fact, it doesn't qualify you for anything. There's a lot more to being a man than good teeth and a hard-on.

I haven't got time to stand around here justifying to you how I choose to live my life in my own home. I you have a problem, pack up your power ties and go look for a woman who'll be happy to scrub the stains out of your shorts. I'm sure there are still plenty of them out there; plenty of women who think love means taking care of junior. Not me! So figure it out.

I'll be home tonight around eight. If you're not here, it's been nice not knowing you. (*She exits.*)